Mercedes L. Norheim
Route #1
Fairfield, Montana

THE AMATEUR CHOIR DIRECTOR

THE AMATEUR CHOIR DIRECTOR

THE AMATEUR
CHOIR DIRECTOR

A Handbook

By

CARL HJORTSVANG

Assistant Professor of Voice and Director of the Choir

EVANSVILLE COLLEGE

ABINGDON-COKESBURY PRESS
NEW YORK • NASHVILLE

THE AMATEUR CHOIR DIRECTOR
COPYRIGHT, MCMXLI
By WHITMORE & STONE

Wartime Books

Wartime shortage of pulp, manpower, and transportation has produced a severe shortage of paper. In compliance with orders of the War Production Board, wartime books are printed on lighter-weight paper. This reduces thickness and weight. New books have more words to the page and smaller margins. This reduces the number of pages without reducing reading content.

Thinner books save paper, critical copper, and other metals. They help also to avoid wartime increases in book prices. Wartime books appear to be smaller, but their content has not been cut. They are complete. The only change is in appearance.

PRINTED IN THE UNITED STATES OF AMERICA

PREFACE

Ordinarily no one will assume leadership of a choir without a genuine interest in the work and without some knowledge of music. However, many entrusted with this responsibility have far too limited equipment beyond these foundation requirements. It is to such potential choir directors that this book is dedicated.

No book can make a director, but it is hoped that this book may help a few to understand and develop the qualities a successful director must have. Included are the fundamentals and some of the finer points of baton technique, also general suggestions for getting the most out of a choir. Many of these fundamentals the author has gleaned from his own experience as director of twelve different amateur choirs.

Carl Hjortsvang

Evansville College
Evansville, Indiana

CONTENTS

7

ILLUSTRATIONS

Chapter 1

THE DIRECTOR

CONDUCTING IS THE ART OF BLENDING THE performance of several players or singers into a harmonious whole. The choir director's task is to concentrate the various purposes of the individual singers into one combined purpose. Thus he has the role of an artist who must play upon an instrument composed of the voices of his choir. True, the instrument itself is human and can perform without a director; yet because of this same human element much is demanded of the director in harmonizing temperaments as well as tones so as to insure a true ensemble.

The performer on a mechanical instrument secures his results through physical control; the director of a choir secures his through remote control dealing with such varying factors as sight, hearing, imitation, and the emotions. It is because of these factors that he needs more than a mere interest in directing, or technical proficiency, or a little musical knowledge, or a good voice. However, because all these qualities can be developed in the average individual, we look forward to a brighter future for our volunteer church choirs.

What most church choirs need now is not necessarily new directors, but only directors who have awakened to the realization that directing is an art, that it is developed through application more than through inspiration, and that the results are well worth the time and effort required.

A choir director's technical "time-beating" ability is only a beginning. The following fundamental requirements we shall consider both to point out their importance and to encourage self-analysis which is logically followed by self-development.

These requirements may be listed as follows:

1. Belief in the mission of music
2. Natural leadership
3. Innate musical ability
4. Personal magnetism
5. Willingness to co-operate
6. Intuitive interpretation
7. A sense of humor
8. Musical scholarship

BELIEF IN THE MISSION OF MUSIC

First of all, a director must believe in the mission of music, not only as an art form, but also as a means of worship. He must have sincere love for the finest music and always strive to present it as perfectly as possible. In addition he must be in sympathy with the work the church is trying to do and desire to help the people through the avenue of music in their religious quest.

A man who thinks of church music only as music will soon have his choir presenting the service as a form of concert. This always leads to self-glorification, a desire to have people say, "Doesn't that choir sing marvelously!" The man who thinks of music as a form of worship is most happy when the people say, "That music brought me closer to God."

The director need not be a member of the church in which he is the music leader; in fact he gets better co-operation often if he is not. But he must be a member of some church and show by his life that he is sincere, that he feels his work is a mission. He must prove that he is a minister of music, not just a hireling who does what he considers to be his job. It is better for the church to select a sincere Christian with little musical experience, but with willingness to learn, rather than to select the world's greatest artist who scoffs at religion. Such a man may develop a marvelous choir, but he will hinder the work of the church, and he had better be in other than church choir work.

NATURAL LEADERSHIP

While natural leadership and intuitive interpretation could be included in personality, they are important enough to be listed separately; and they are traits which are capable of independent development.

The choir director must be confident of his leadership ability. He must be assertive, but not dictatorial. If he lacks self-confidence, he must take care that those vibrations do not reach his group. He must be recognized as the sole leader during both rehearsals and performances, and he must assume that this leadership is expected of him. Such co-operation molds the group into a homogeneous whole which can perform as one voice; without it, results are left to chance. The director then becomes a follower of the accompanist or of some strong-voiced or strong-willed individual, and he will be fortunate if he long has a choir at all.

An authority on conducting divides this sense of leadership into three elements: (1) confidence in one's general ability and in one's knowledge of the subject being handled; (2) the ability to make oneself understood; and (3) a tremendous love and respect for the thing being done, this latter including a love for music in general, choral music in particular, and each individual anthem or special musical number that is attempted.[1]

INNATE MUSICAL ABILITY

The director must have innate musical ability. He cannot depend upon his accompanist to determine the rhythm and to maintain it, nor upon his singers for evaluation and interpretation. To be a successful leader he must have a strong rhythmic sense, a pleasing though not necessarily a trained voice, ability to read notes moderately well, and a feeling for good music. He must be deeply responsive when good music is well performed. If the director cannot feel rhythm, he cannot beat time; if he does not respond to good music, neither his choir nor his audience will be moved similarly as he directs it.

On the other hand, the director need not be a musical genius. Many examples from musical history prove that innate musical ability alone does not make a good director. The famous composers, Berlioz, Massenet, and Saint-Saens were not considered good directors; and Dr. Philipp Spitta, an eminent historian and critic, comments as follows upon Schumann as a conductor:

Schumann was wholly wanting in real talent for con-

---

[1] Karl Wilson Gehrkins, *Essentials in Conducting*, Oliver Ditson Co., 1919, pp. 15-19.

ducting; all who ever saw him conduct or played under his direction are agreed on this point. Irrespective of the fact that conducting for any length of time tired him out, he had neither the collectedness and prompt presence of mind, nor the sympathetic faculty, nor the enterprising dash, without each of which conducting in the true sense is impossible. He even found difficulty in starting at a given tempo; nay, he sometimes shrank from giving any initial beat, so that some energetic pioneer would begin without waiting for the signal, and without incurring Schumann's wrath! Besides this, any thorough practice, bit by bit, with his orchestra, with instructive remarks by the way as to the mode of execution, was impossible to this great artist, who in this respect was a striking contrast to Mendelssohn. He would have a piece played through, and if it did not answer to his wishes, have it repeated. If it went no better the second or perhaps third time, he would be extremely angry at what he considered the clumsiness, or even the ill-will of the players; but detailed remarks he never made.[2]

This should give encouragement to those who are not musical geniuses. What may be lacking in the field of creative ability can be made up in other fields. If the would-be director has general musical knowledge, with hard work and application he can go far.

---

[2] From Dr. Spitta's article on Schumann in *Grove's Dictionary of Music and Musicians*, published by The Macmillan Co.

PERSONAL MAGNETISM

By personal magnetism we mean a strong and pleasing personality. The person who lacks these qualities and antagonizes others will make a failure of directing.

The director might be called a "democratic dictator," for he must dominate his choir, yet it must be only because of the willingness of the singers to be thus ruled. He must have such sincerity and honesty of character that he will hold the respect of his group whether or not they always agree with his opinions or interpretations.

This quality of personal magnetism, or personality, is the one over which an individual has the least control. If he lacks it, he will need to spend much time and effort in order to develop it; "for personality is the general inclination of the sum total of individual conduct." [3] It can be called the epitome of one's self. However, careful self-analysis plus self-control can do wonders in this psychological field. It can make a leader of almost anyone who is honest enough to admit his deficiencies and who will strive persistently to correct them.

The test of a director's personality is his ability to maintain the friendly co-operation of his full membership.

---

[3] L. R. Coleman and S. Commins, *Psychology, a Simplification*, p. 75.

WILLINGNESS TO CO-OPERATE

Since the performance of good church music is not an end in itself, but rather is a means for inculcating and aiding in religious worship, the director must co-operate with the minister and be willing to receive suggestions on correlating the music with the rest of the service. This relationship between minister and director must be reciprocal, and each must be willing to give in when necessary in order that everything may work out smoothly. The special music should fit the theme of the sermon or of the scripture lesson, if not in exact words, then at least in mood. But amateur choirs are often limited in the variety of music they can perform, and for this reason it may be necessary to make certain concessions. Sometimes it is desirable to have the anthem appear at a different point in the service (a prayer anthem appearing before or after a prayer, a scriptural anthem appearing after a scripture reading), thus giving both minister and director more leeway in maintaining a unified service.

The director has a twofold objective. He must present certain types of music when he feels his choir is best able to present them, and he must try to give the church (as represented by the minister) the type of music that is desired each Sunday. It may sound simple, but in practice it is difficult and can be accomplished only when a spirit of co-operation prevails.

INTUITIVE INTERPRETATION

Intuitive interpretation follows the composer's thought at least in a measure. A director with intuition mentally hears a composition well performed and then devises the means for securing such results. He must not be satisfied merely with having his choir sing louder in one place and softer in another; he must reach down to the emotional content of the composition until his singers feel that emotion and express it. They must feel the joy that the composer felt and share his burden of sin or sorrow. Then with a little directing their voices will take on the needed color and volume. Their great need is to feel intuitively what the composer felt and to try to express those emotions as he expressed them.

A SENSE OF HUMOR

The director of an amateur choir indeed needs a sense of humor. This is of great help in maintaining a proper sense of values for both the director and the performers. Mistakes are bound to be made. If these are pointed out in a way to bring a laugh, often the ones responsible will try to do better; but if the director's manner intimates, "Don't you know better than to make such a mistake?" a feeling of resentment may be created which will cause the offenders to remain silent instead of trying again. If something humorous happens and the choir members laugh, not only let them laugh, but laugh with them. A laugh expressed creates good will; a laugh repressed engenders bitterness.

On the other hand, a choir rehearsal is serious business which can be harmed by too much levity. If the rehearsal does not accomplish its primary purpose, it is a failure; but it must be remembered that in a volunteer group interest and good will are the adhesives that hold it together and that these elements must be maintained at all costs.

Remember always that a laugh must be with the singers and not at them. There must be no sarcasm, or condescension, but rather a feeling that the director is enjoying the rehearsal and that he hopes the choir members are also. While there may be many rehearsals in which there are no general laughs, yet if some smiles have not been near the surface, then it is very likely that some scowls have been.

Probably the greatest need for a sense of humor arises when the director thinks of his own importance. He must, as was stated before, have confidence in himself; but it never pays to take himself too seriously. If he does, petty annoyances will become magnified and seem insurmountable. A difficulty met with a smile often proves to be no difficulty at all.

MUSICAL SCHOLARSHIP

Musical scholarship is listed last because scholarship cannot help a director much without the other qualities. If he lacks a pleasing personality, even though he has great musical knowledge, he will not be admired by his choir; without a sense of leadership he cannot advance far; neither can one who lacks an intuitive sense get the best results from a volunteer group.

A man who is by way of becoming a great director will never cease developing himself. He will hear concerts given by other choirs; he will study new music continually; he will seize every opportunity for all-around development. The better director he is, the more anxious he will be to extend his knowledge in both the theory and the practice of music. Everyone who studies pays himself the compliment of thinking he has the ability to develop. Those who do so persistently will some day be receiving compliments from others.

Chapter 2

THE TECHNIQUE OF THE BATON

THIS CHAPTER PRESENTS CONDUCTING FROM THE viewpoint of the director who stands before his group, and not from that of an organist-director or singer-director. This latter is treated in Chapter VI. However, even for the organist-director and the singer-director the technique of handling a baton is an essential foundation which will prove its usefulness many times when *a cappella* music is attempted or when music expressive of deep feeling is rehearsed.

Even though a director intends to conduct his group by use of hand gestures alone, he should begin his training with a baton. For one reason, it gives him something to hold, a foil, which reduces the self-consciousness aroused when something new is begun. Also it will train him to keep his hands in front of himself. This factor should be stressed. An orchestra may be seated in a U shape about the conductor, and thus require more gestures to the sides; but the choir is placed in front of the director and can see motions made in front of him better than those made at the sides; thus he will be more easily understood by the choir and less conspicuous to the audience, which means they will both more readily catch the message of the music. Directing done at the sides, especially without a baton, often looks like an imitation of a bird with fluttering wings.

This initial use of the baton will give the director a more flexible wrist, thus enabling him to secure smoother legato from the singers. Then, too, it provides a better chance to consider the directional qualities of the beats.

THE DIRECTIONAL QUALITY OF BEATS

Beats, as outlined by modern measure structure, require a definite direction of baton movement.[1] This directional quality has become standardized through use, and forms the foundation of conventional baton technique.

The first beat of the measure is always down, no matter how many or how few beats the measure contains. The last beat of the measure has an upward swing. Thus the first beat, while not always receiving the greatest accent, is still represented by the lowest point that the baton reaches, while the last beat is represented by the highest point the baton reaches —except for the continued swing of the baton in preparation for the first or down beat. (See Figure 7.)

---

[1] See W. Earhart, *The Eloquent Baton*, M. Whitmark & Sons, 1931, p. 1.

The direction of the intermediary beats depends upon the number of beats in the measure. In three-pulse rhythm, a swing or beat to the right is added between the down and the up beat. In four-pulse rhythm, a swing or beat to the left is added to what we already have in the three-pulse rhythm. This swing to the left comes before the swing to the right.

All rhythms—even 5/4 and 7/4—are fundamentally based upon a two-, three-, or four-pulse measure; and thus all the directional qualities of the beats can be worked out from the above foundation.

THE USE OF THE BATON

The baton should be a light-weight, slender stick about fourteen to eighteen inches in length, and a little heavier at the end that is held than at the tip.

Hold the baton in the right hand with all four fingers curved about it and the thumb pressed against it pointing toward the tip. (See Figures 1 and 2.)

Fig. 1—Holding the Baton   Fig. 2—Holding the Baton

The tightness with which the baton is held will vary

with the emotion of the composition directed. For average compositions it should be held lightly by the tips of the fingers much as a violin bow is held. (Figure 2.)

At first most of the motion imparted to the baton should come through loose wrist movement, with just a little of the movement coming from the forearm. The emotion of the composition directed will determine the looseness of the wrist and the size of the stroke. These factors will be considered in the chapter dealing with interpretation.

As beginning exercises, the following should be used:

Exercise 1. Hold the baton lightly as shown in Figure 2. Grasp the forearm firmly with the left hand so that all baton movements will be given by the wrist only. Then make the tip of the baton move up and down over a distance of about fifteen inches. (Figure 3.)

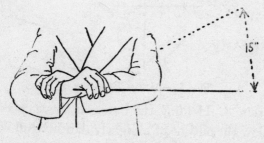

Fig. 3—Baton Exercise 1

Exercise 2. Holding the baton in the same manner as above, make the tip follow a triangular pattern of down, right, up (Figure 4).

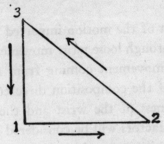

Fig. 4.—Baton Exercise 2

Exercise 3. Holding the baton as above, make the tip follow the outline of an angular figure 8 (Figure 5). The motion is down, left, right, up, using the count 1, 2, 3, 4.

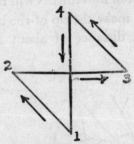

Fig. 5.—Baton Exercise 3

Exercise 4. Holding the baton as above, make the tip follow the outline of a slightly slanting and rounded figure 8 (Figure 6), using the count 1, 2.

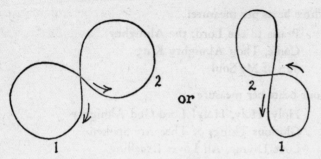

FIG. 6.—BATON EXERCISE 4

These exercises should not be done jerkily, but as smoothly as possible, with the wrist moving loosely. There should be no hesitation at the points where the count is given, but only the infinitesimal pause necessary to change the direction in which the baton is traveling. The exercises should be practiced at various tempos, both slow and fast, and should be persisted in until any one of the patterns can be followed both accurately and fluently. If it is possible to have these various rhythms played while the exercises are being practiced, greater benefit will be derived. No retards or holds should be observed in these exercises. Recommended hymns containing no rhythmical variations which could be used for this purpose are the following.

Two beats per measure:

    Now Praise We All Our God

    Joy to the World

    Holy Spirit from on High

Three beats per measure:

> Praise to the Lord, the Almighty
> Come, Thou Almighty King
> Sun of My Soul

Four beats per measure:

> Holy, Holy, Holy! Lord God Almighty
> Glorious Things of Thee Are Spoken
> Love Divine, All Loves Excelling
> Saviour, Again to Thy Dear Name We Raise
> Abide with Me
> Hark! the Herald Angels Sing

As soon as the exercises outlined above have been well practiced and the wrist has developed freedom, the exercises should be done again in the following manner:

Make the pattern the baton follows more florid by giving each beat a little more accent and making the wrist and baton bounce back after each beat as though the wrist were moved by a spring which checked any far motion from the center and brought it back again. The outlines which the tip of the baton then follows will be approximately as shown in Figures 7, 8, and 9.

Remember that these exercises are to be done with the left hand holding the right forearm stationary. After fluency and flexibility of wrist have been gained, then the forearm should be given freedom to move; but the average movement should not be more than from two to four inches except in the case of selections requiring a vigorous type of conducting.

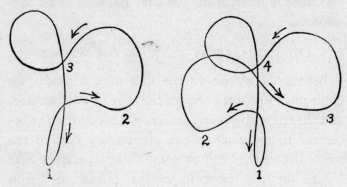

FIG. 7.—3/4 BEAT OUTLINE. FIG. 8.—4/4 BEAT OUTLINE

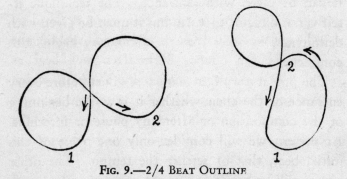

FIG. 9.—2/4 BEAT OUTLINE

These florid patterns as practiced in this manner, allowing the forearm to move, form the outlines of the movement the hand and the baton go through in the actual conducting of a choir in rehearsal and in performance. Variations occur only in order to indicate expression and modifications in the rhythm. Use these motions as the fundamental basis of all conducting.

THE PREPARATORY BEAT, OR THE ATTACK

Before the attack on the first note is made, the choir must know the tempo, the type of tone wanted, and the strength of tone necessary. All this can be indicated to the choir in one preparatory beat of the baton before the choir enters. This preparatory beat is one of the most important phases of baton technique and will require diligent practice before it can be given with assurance. The technique itself is not difficult to learn, but it must be given with definiteness in order that the choir may begin with confidence.

The preparatory beat should be given before every entrance of the choir whether it is at the beginning of the composition or after any pause or interlude. At present we will consider only one phase of this initial beat, that of setting the tempo. The other phases will be considered in the chapter dealing with expression.

The preliminary position to be adopted by the conductor before the start of any composition, no matter what its nature or on what beat of the measure it starts, is always the same. (For choral numbers we infer that there has been no instrumental introduction.) The assuming of this position means "get ready," and should receive immediate attention from all the members of the group. (See Figure 12 or Figure 13, pages 51 and 52.)

The preparatory beat motion occupies the time value of one full beat in the rhythm of the composition being performed (the beat ahead of the opening note or opening accented note), and is most easily made and understood if it is given its full directional quality.

The first practice should be in compositions beginning on the first beat of a measure. Use any of the hymns suggested on pages 27 and 28. The motion the hand and the tip of the baton go through is indicated in Figure 10.

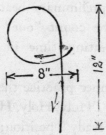

FIG. 10.—THE ATTACK GESTURE

Measurements are given in inches for the hand, not the tip of the baton, to follow. But these are to be considered as proportions rather than actual measurements, after the motion has been learned, for the size of the motions is influenced by several factors which will be discussed later. It will be noted that the motion is exactly the same as that covered from beat three to beat one in 3/4 time (Figure 7) or the same as from beat four to beat one in 4/4 time (Figure 8).

Practice this preliminary beat, or upbeat, as it is often called, in both slow and fast rhythms, thinking of definite songs that start in this manner of both 3/4 and 4/4 rhythm. For a song in 3/4 rhythm (try "America") hold the hand in position of Figure 12; then count one, two, three, in the tempo in which the song should be sung. Hold the hand steady while you count one, two, then at "three" begin the motion which forms the preliminary beat arriving at 1 in Figure 7, when the count "one" is reached again. Then continue beating time in the regular 3/4 rhythm pattern.

In the same manner practice the preliminary beat for a 4/4 song (try "Holy, Holy, Holy!"). Hold the hand in the "get ready" position; count one, two, three, in the tempo of the piece; at "four" begin the preparatory movement; and at "one" have the hand at the bottom of the stroke and begin singing, continuing to beat time in the 4/4 rhythmic pattern. Instead of counting, you might try humming the first measure of the melody before making the preliminary beat. This may make the rhythm more clearly felt in your mind. It must be remembered that counting or humming are merely temporary expedients to help you feel the rhythm while you are learning. If later you feel that they are necessary to bolster your self-confidence, they must then be done silently.

After smoothness and confidence have been gained, secure someone to play the piano, or to sing the melody for you. Have him start the hymns as you give him the preliminary beats. That will be the best practice you can get and will check on whether or not you are definitely establishing the desired rhythm.

After these exercises have been thoroughly mastered, then try to start hymns that begin on other than the first beat of the measure, such as the following.

3/4 time:
   O Worship the King
   Blest Be the Tie That Binds
   O Come, O Come, Immanuel
   All the Way My Saviour Leads Me

4/4 time:
   O Day of Rest and Gladness

> All Hail the Power of Jesus Name
> O Little Town of Bethlehem
> He Leadeth Me
> I Love to Tell the Story

The principle of the preparatory beat is the same in every case. To begin a song that starts on the third beat of 3/4 rhythm, hold the hand in the "get ready" position and count one, two, three; on "one" the hand is steady, at "two" the hand moves to position 2 in Figure 7, and then continues at a curve upward to 3, arriving there at count "three," at which point the first note of the song begins. You will notice that the hand has given one beat previous to the entrance note of the piece following the regular 3/4 rhythmic pattern. After the song is begun, this rhythmic pattern continues. In the same manner, to begin on the fourth beat of a song in 4/4 rhythm, hold the hand in the "get ready" position, and count one, two, three, four, moving the arm to the right for "three" and curving upward for "four," where the song begins, and then down for "one," and on in the regular 4/4 rhythm.

The principle is the same in beginning a song on any other beat of the measure. The hand would be held in the "get ready" position, and would then fall into the rhythmic pattern of the song one beat ahead of the entrance of the voice.

The hardest type of entrance to get a group to come in on is that which has a pickup note, that is, an entrance note or group of notes of less than one count value. The choir will ordinarily have to be drilled in an entrance of this kind. The directing itself is simple enough. The preliminary beat is given in the usual manner as though these pickup notes were not there; that is, only one beat is given ahead of the first note appearing on a beat. The pickup notes are to be sung during this preliminary beat.

For emphasis, this preliminary beat technique may be summarized as follows:

1. Hold the "get ready" position shown in Figure 12 or 13.

2. Be sure that every member of your group can and does see you and is prepared to begin.

3. Mentally count the preliminary part of the measure or hum (mentally) the first measure of the song. (This need be done only until you have confidence in yourself to start the song smoothly.)

4. Give the preparatory beat in the tempo which you have established in your mind by your silent counting.

5. Be sure your choir enters together at the right moment.

6. Continue beating time, following the rhythmic pattern of the tempo in which the piece is written.

THE RELEASE

Almost as important as starting a composition is ending it.   There is special technique that must be learned in order that the cutoff may be clean-cut and incisive.

The general procedure is as follows: As the last note is sung let the baton and arm fall into approximately the same position they had for the "get ready" position.   A little higher and a little more to the right will be just as satisfactory.   The baton should go to this position instead of the position it would otherwise go to on that beat in following its usual rhythmic pattern.

The baton is held in this position during the time it is desired that the final note should be held.   Then just one beat before the note should be released, the hand and baton are lifted slightly to the right as a warning gesture and then brought down diagonally in front of the body to end the tone.   This bringing of the hand across diagonally indicates that the rhythm or tone is cut, as nowhere else in our rhythmic pattern does this diagonal gesture occur.   The tone should end simultaneously with the hand reaching the bottom of this diagonal stroke.

Chapter 3

INDICATING EXPRESSION

SO FAR WE HAVE CONSIDERED THE BARE FUNDA-
mentals of conducting, namely the use of the baton
in what is really its least essential phase. It is true that
beating time to the rhythm is important and should
be thoroughly mastered before this chapter is ap-
proached; but from now on that phase of conducting
should be done subconsciously in order that the mind
may be occupied with the problem of how to get the
most out of the piece, how to get the most out of the
choir, and how to make the music really live for the
audience.

To get the most out of the piece, the conductor
must have studied it thoroughly so that he knows
what he wants in the way of tempo, volume, variations in volume, tone quality, accents, and other expression details. Second, he must know how to indicate to the choir what he wants. Third, he must
be able to train his choir so that it will give him what
he wants when he is directing. Unfortunately, most
singers in volunteer choirs do not know how to make
a true soft tone, a musical sounding loud tone, how
to make nuances, how to enunciate clearly, or many

other of the details that mark the difference between usual singing and "good" singing. The purpose of this chapter is to present the technique of indicating expression. A later chapter will deal with the singers themselves.

TEMPO

Tempo is so important that we must place it first in discussing the various divisions of expression, for tempo determines the value and effect of the other divisions, even though it is not as effective in this way as Richard Wagner believed:

> The whole duty of the conductor is comprised in his ability always to indicate the right tempo. His choice of tempo will show whether he understands the piece or not . . .[1]

While the director will find that true tempo does not necessarily induce correct force and expression, yet it makes these other features of expression more easy; and conversely, the wrong tempo can nullify the effect of other features of expression. First let us determine the means of ascertaining the correct tempo.

Here are five helps in determining tempo as listed by one conductor:

---

[1] *On Conducting.*

1. The metronome indication, found at the beginning of most modern scores.

2. The tempo or mood expressions (*Andante, Allegro,* etc.).

3. The general spirit of the text.

4. Tradition.

5. Individual judgment of tempo depending upon the "quality" of the music.[2]

Of all of these, individual judgment is the most important. But let the reasons be strong and sound before any great deviation is made from a tempo indicated by any of the previous headings.

Metronomic indications are found at the beginning of most pieces of music now written. Examples of metronomic marks: M. M. 62 or = 62. The number stands for the number of beats per minute. If there is a note ahead of the number, that indicates the type of note receiving one beat. This tempo indication is placed there for a purpose, but never adopt that tempo merely because it is the suggested one. You must feel that the tempo is right before you can interpret the piece satisfactorily. If your judgment, after analyzing the number, tells you that another tempo is better, then by all means adopt that one. Yet remember that changing something merely to be different, or to show your own originality, is not musicianship. Be sure your changes are based on musically sound reasons.

[2] Karl Wilson Gehrkins, *Essentials in Conducting,* Oliver Ditson Co., 1919,

Many pieces have only Italian terms to indicate the suggested tempo and expression. There is a tendency to use English expressions in some of the newer compositions; but Italian has been a universal musical language, and any person scorning these terms because they are Italian is as foolish as a doctor would be who scorned Latin medical terms. It will pay to have a dictionary of musical terms on hand. A few are listed below, indicating relative tempo only and depending upon the performer for exact interpretation. In some cases both the tempo and the mood are expressed in the same word.

	Lento—slow
	Largo—slow, broad
Slow:	*Larghetto*—not as slow as *Largo*
	Adagio—at ease
	Grave—with gravity, heavy
	Andante—walking, going
	Andantino—usually faster than *andante* (sometimes slower)
Medium:	
	Moderato—moderately, at a moderate pace
	Allegretto—a little slower than *allegro*
	Allegro—cheerful, lively
Fast:	*Con moto*—with motion
	Vivace—vivaciously
	Presto—quick

A few modifying expressions also should be known:

Molto—very much

Assai—very

Poco—a little

Piu—more (*Piu mosso* a little faster)

Meno—less (*meno mosso*—a little slower)

Ma non tanto—but not so much

Ma non troppo—but not too much

The general spirit of the text combined with the feeling aroused by the harmonic structure of the music is the true source of correct tempo. It is as Mathis Lussy says:

> The normal tempo . . . . can never be the result of arbitrary rules, and depends neither upon the composer nor the performer. In fact, the true tempo of a composition, that which . . . . most exactly interprets its inmost thought, is the tempo which results from its actual structure.[3]

Thus it is in the composition itself that the conductor finds his tempo mark rather than in the instructions at the beginning.

Tradition does not play the important part in music that it formerly played. It has become almost a modern precept to violate tradition. Beware of falling into this attitude. Be sure to find as far as possible the traditional interpretation of your compositions. (This, of course, applies especially to the old classics such as *The Messiah* and *Elijah*. The book

---

[3] *Musical Expression.*

Choral Technique and Interpretation by Coward is the best source of *Messiah* interpretation.)

On every possible occasion listen to other choirs both over the radio and at programs that can be attended. Then evaluate the interpretation of the numbers sung, always considering the musical background of the director and the ability of his choir in order to judge the true worth of his interpretation.

But, again, never adopt an interpretation just because someone else has used it even though he has the backing of tradition. Neither discard that interpretation because someone has done it that way. Adopt the tempo (and interpretation) that in your judgment, after thorough study and analysis, seems best.

VARIATIONS IN TEMPO

In the chapter dealing with the technique of the baton we discussed beating time in various rhythms. The beginning director will find a variation of tempo creeping in without his intending that it should do so. For example, there is a subconscious tendency to slow down when singing softly and to speed up when singing louder. This tendency must be guarded against. Careful baton practice with a metronome will help to establish a feeling of steady rhythm.

There are times, however, when a change of rhythm is definitely desired. Usually the composer indicates these changes; but occasionally the director himself will wish to vary the rhythm. Some of the Italian terms used to indicate this change of rhythm follow:

A gradual slowing of tempo:
Ritardando
Rallentando

An immediate slowing of tempo:
Piu lento
Ritenuto
Meno mosso

A gradual slowing with a crescendo:
Allargando (becoming broad)

A gradual slowing with a decrescendo:
Morendo
Smorzando (gradually dying away)

A gradual increase in tempo:
Accelerando (Accel.)
Stringendo
Poco a poco animato

An immediate increase in tempo:
Piu allegro or *Piu animato*
Piu mosso

The usual definition of rhythm is, "A regularly recurring succession of beats, sounds, or motions." If instead we consider rhythm to be a flow of motion with regularly occurring pulses, we have a truer picture and find it easier to make smooth variations in the spacing of these recurring pulses, for the space between the pulses is as much a part of rhythm as is the pulse itself. Even a hold is merely a lengthening of the space between pulses, rather than a stopping of the rhythm. Direct the composition as a flowing melody, not as something to be counted out: one, two, three, one, etc. As soon as this is really felt, a greater smoothness will develop in the directing both of a steady rhythm and of tempo nuances, and also in the performance of the singers. If this most important smoothness is kept in mind, there is no great difficulty in the actual directing of these tempo variations. Ordinarily it is well to use both hands in directing changes, as this holds the attention a little better.

A gradual increase in the tempo should be carried out with a sharper "hit" of the baton at the accent points and less florid motions between them; a gradual slowing of the tempo will be treated in the opposite way.

There are times when slight nuances are desirable in the flow of the rhythm. Even when they are not indicated, they add much to the interpretation. They must be used sparingly and cautiously, however; but they have their place in emotional music. For example, a feeling of heaviness or weariness is increased when the tempo is held back slightly and a feeling of joy or lightness results when the tempo is slightly increased. But always remember that the rhythm must be a smooth flow, and any slight variation must not break this smoothness. As in retards and accelerandos, both hands should be used for directing nuances. In slowing down, the motions are made more florid or flowing, and in speeding up, more direct and accented.

THE HOLD

There are two types of hold; in one the rhythm is merely held back, and the tone continues unbroken after the hold is released, while in the other the rhythm and the tone are broken and pick up anew after the hold has been released. These two types of hold are handled somewhat differently, although the principle is the same. In either case a preparatory beat is given before the beginning, or the continuation, of the next tone.

First let us consider the hold after which the tone is broken. No matter upon which beat of the measure it occurs, it is treated in the same manner. Holds of this type are directed exactly the same as the release mentioned in the previous chapter. If the hold is merely the end of a phrase, and the song continues immediately, the cutoff motion ending the tone also re-establishes the rhythmic feeling, since it is given in the rhythm of the song and serves as the count before the entrance of the voices. The baton then falls into the old rhythmic pattern on the next beat, the voices picking up at that point. The counting could be illustrated by the second measure of "Old Hundredth" (Doxology). One, two, three-e-e-e-e, three, four, one.

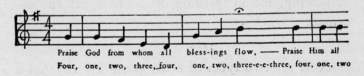

Praise God from whom all   bless-ings flow, —— Praise Him all
Four, one, two, three, four,   one, two, three-e-e-three, four, one, two

FIG. 11.—COUNTING FOR A HOLD

If this rhythm is sung at metronome setting 60, that is, sixty counts a minute, each note would be held for one second except the notes with holds. Each syllable of "blessings" would be held for one second, "flow" would be held during the third and fourth seconds, being cut off at the beginning of the fifth, and "praise" would be sung at the beginning of the sixth. (For the purpose of illustration I am placing an arbitrary time value upon the hold.) The baton would be held stationary during the third second, would begin the cutoff motion at the fourth second, be at the bottom of the cutoff motion at the fifth second, and giving beat four at the sixth second. If the hold were to be longer, the timing of the cutoff motion and the picking up of the next note would still be the same.

If a longer silent pause is at any time desired after the hold has been cut off, the baton would be held at rest at the point it reached at the bottom of the cut-off stroke during the time silence was desired, and then a new pickup gesture would be performed.

Examples of holds occuring on various beats of the measure will be found in the following hymns:

First beat: A Mighty Fortress Is Our God
Second beat: I Hear Thy Welcome Voice
                While Shepherds Watched Their Flocks
Third beat: Tell Me the Old, Old Story

Holds after which the tone is not cut off but continues unbroken into the following notes are handled as follows: The baton falls into the position indicating the tone is to be held and retains this position during the indicated time, and then a pickup gesture is performed for the next note (without the cutoff), the singers continuing without having stopped the tone. The purpose of the pickup gesture is to give warning to the singers and to indicate the tempo, which must be reestablished for them.

In order to emphasize the difference in the two

styles of holds, try conducting some of the above hymns in this manner, tying over two phrases without taking a breath at the end of the hold.

In consecutive holds, as in the fourth measure of the chorus of "Softly and Tenderly Jesus Is Calling," the baton is lifted up at the end of each hold and then brought back to the same position to indicate a new hold. Make these motions rather slowly, allowing at least a second and a half for each one. At the end of the third hold make the cutoff gesture. The next to the last measure of the chorus is easily handled if the baton is used to indicate each note instead of each beat.

DYNAMICS

The word dynamics means the loudness or softness of tones, and the amount of accent they should receive. Almost the same five factors could be used in determining the dynamics of the composition that were applied to determining the tempo; therefore this discussion will concern itself only with the second point, namely Italian mood indications and expression marks. These are found at the beginning and throughout most compositions. Only a few can be given here.

Soft: *Pianississimo* (*ppp*) very, very softly
         Pianissimo (*pp*) very softly
         Piano (*p*) softly

Medium: *Mezzo piano* (*mp*) moderately soft
           Mezzo forte (*mf*) moderately loud
Loud: *Forte* (*f*) loud
           Fortissimo (*ff*) very loud
           Fortississimo (*fff*) very, very loud

Becoming gradually louder:
           Crescendo (*Cresc.*)

Becoming gradually softer:
           Decrescendo (*Decresc.*)
           Diminuendo (*Dim.*)

Other common expression marks:
           Dolce—sweetly
           Con amore—with tenderness
           Expressivo—with expression
           Sforzando (*sf*) or *Forzato* (*fz*) an extra accent to be applied to one note or a chord, the amount of the accent depending upon the character of the piece.

It is evident that these terms are relative only, and the exact shading is left to the judgment of the director. The composer can give suggestions, but the director is the interpreter who must decide the value of each term, and must use shading of his own where specific directions are not given. In all cases let the feeling of the text and the flow of the music determine the strength of the tone and the strength of the accent. Seek variety of tone in order to maintain interest in the composition and to drive home its message, but never use any form of interpretation merely to show what "effects" your choir can give. That brands you as a "show-off" and usually spoils the emotional atmosphere the music should create.

Soft singing should be directed with smaller motions than loud singing. The baton should be held lightly with the tips of the fingers as shown in Figure 2. As the tone becomes louder the fingers will close more firmly about the baton, and for very loud singing, the baton will be held tightly in the fist as shown in Figure 1. The louder the tone desired, the bigger and more sweeping the motions made by the director. The director will probably feel this subconsciously, and certainly the choir will respond to what it sees, usually without having to be told the difference. Most choirs have to be trained to sing softly. They respond quickly when asked to sing loudly, but do not soften half enough when asked to sing pianissimo. Individual accents are indicated by a sharper "hit" of the baton at the point needing accent.

It is well to use the left hand as a help in indicating the volume desired, and to control a change of volume. If a composition should be started with a soft tone, let the baton be held lightly with the right hand, and the left hand held at about the same level as the baton with the palm downward, as in Figure 12. The pickup gesture should be small, given with a very flexible wrist. It may be given with both hands, in which case the choir usually will come in

FIG. 12.—POSITION TO INDICATE SOFT SINGING

with a firmer and slightly louder tone than if the left hand remained stationary as though warning against singing too loudly.

If the beginning is to be made with loud tones, the baton should be grasped firmly, the left hand held in the same position as mentioned before, but with the palm turned inward and almost upward, the hands held farther apart than for a soft start, and the pick-up gesture made vigorously and broadly with both hands. See Figure 13.

FIG. 13.—POSITION TO INDICATE LOUD SINGING

The crescendo should be directed with the baton gradually making bigger and bigger motions, usually with the beats more clearly marked. If it is to be comparatively rapid, the left hand should beat out the rhythm also, for both hands will draw better results from the choir than one hand alone would do. However, if the crescendo is to be gradual, it is better for the left hand to control the choir by indicating by the way the hand is held whether the increase of tone is right or not. Turning the palm upward means increase the volume a little faster; bringing the hand upward gradually, or motioning a little toward the body as though beckoning for them to come closer will increase the volume still more rapidly. To slow up the crescendo the hand need merely turn slightly as though in warning.

A diminuendo should be directed with the baton gradually making smaller and smaller motions, diminishing the accents on the beats as well. As with the crescendo, the left hand should help indicate what is wanted. It may either beat out the rhythm together with the right hand, or it may serve as a control of the decrescendo. The palm held toward the choir indicates softer tones. If a more rapid softening is desired, the hand may motion toward the choir slightly as though to quiet it. If the softening is too rapid, the hand may turn slightly inward, if necessary, even with palm almost upward, till the right response is received.

There are other ways of indicating and controlling crescendos and diminuendos, but I have found that choirs recognize this type of gesture without being told, whereas with other types they often have to be coached as to their meaning. This type of left hand gesture is especially fitting when the directing is entirely by hand.

Often a small nuance, that is, a crescendo and a diminuendo occurring on one, two, or three notes is very effective. Sometimes they are marked thus <>, and sometimes they are not marked at all but would be effective if used. Be careful to make them delicately, for too much of a crescendo will spoil the effect entirely. A nuance of this type may be indicated almost entirely by the left hand which should turn palm upward, perhaps with an upward motion to indicate the crescendo, and then turn palm inward and downward to indicate the diminuendo. The right hand may help indicate the nuance by making a somewhat larger sweep on the beat or beats where the crescendo occurs. Moving the hands first farther apart and then closer together also helps indicate an increase and then a decrease of tone.

MOOD

All vocal music can be divided into two types according to mood. One type is subjective, and the other is objective. Music which is devotional, or that which deals with a state of mind such as sorrow, repentance, or love is classed as subjective music. That which deals with external subjects or facts is classed as objective. For example, the hymn "Lead, Kindly Light" is subjective, and "Praise to the Lord, the Almighty" is objective.

Another classification of vocal music must be made according to the type of treatment it should receive, namely, lyric or dramatic. The lyric style is very smooth and connected, while the dramatic style is bold and with accent.

Subjective music should nearly always be treated lyrically. Objective music should nearly always be treated dramatically. Lyric treatment will be indicated to the choir when the baton is held lightly in the fingers as indicated in Figure 2, showing that the tone is light and flowing. The gestures should be flowing, with the wrist very flexible. This does not mean that lyric singing must be soft; indeed, it is possible to use almost full volume, yet although directing motions become large and the tone big, the light holding of the baton and its flowing motions indicate a connected flowing tone.

Dramatic treatment is indicated by holding the baton firmly in the hand as shown in Figure 1. The beat outline is given more firmly and with less florid motions, indicating that a strong, incisive tone is wanted. On the whole, dramatic treatment requires more volume than lyric treatment, although there are exceptions. Remember also that a composition may be lyric or subjective in some parts and dramatic or objective in others.

TIMBRE

We have discussed lyric and dramatic tones and how to indicate that such tones are wanted. The next thing is to suggest a few ways to get these tones from the choir. Singing cannot be taught from a book, and especially not from a short chapter such as this one must be. All one can do is to give the few suggestions that appear now in Chapter V with the hope that they will help overcome some of the faults that beset amateur voices and amateur choirs.

The foundation of good singing is good breathing. If the choir is taught diaphragmatic breathing, the possibilities of tone quality, tone control, and tonal technique will be greatly enhanced.

It is natural to breathe correctly, and anyone watching a baby breathe will be able to see the correct way. Yet as we mature we depart from this natural method because of our posture as we lean over a desk or because of nervous tension. Probably four out of five people breathe only with the upper part of their lungs (lift the shoulders or the upper part of the chest). This type of breathing utilizes about half of the breath capacity; it causes a tenseness of the throat which hinders good singing; and it creates a hard quality which is especially noticeable on high tones.

Diaphragmatic breathing means deep breathing. This requires first of all a good posture. Stand erect with the weight on the balls of the feet, chest medium high, the shoulders at rest, and the neck free from tension, so that the head may move freely in any direction. Then place one hand over the diaphragm just above the waist line and place the other hand on the upper chest. As a breath is inhaled, the hand over the diaphragm is pushed outward while the hand on the upper chest remains stationary. The expansion of the body wall at the diaphragm which pushed the hand forward is the result of diaphragmatic breathing. This expansion will be noticed in the normal breathing of any infant and in adults when they can relax. Any sleeping person breathes diaphragmatically. For singing purposes the breath taken should be greater and therefore the expansion also somewhat greater than would occur in normal breathing. During the time a singing tone is held the expansion remains, sinking in only gradually, because the diaphragm is used to control the outward flow of breath as long as the tone is held. The Chicago Council of Singing Teachers states it as follows:

The diaphragm remains vitalized during exhalation, while the whole lower torso, including the intercostal, the lumbar, and the abdominal muscles participate in the flexible support of tone. This condition should be interpreted as flexible activity, and any rigidity carefully avoided.[4]

Give your choir training in this type of breathing. You will be fortunate if most of the members can learn it; but even a few members breathing correctly will help much in the quality of the singing. In a lyric style of tone the flow will be much smoother and sweeter if the breath is diaphragmatically controlled. In a dramatic tone the intensity and volume will be much greater; and the high notes made with

---

[4] In a leaflet, "Statement of Vocal Principles, Breathing."

breath coming from the diaphragm will be fuller and freer, giving more pleasure both to the singer and the listener. For methods of correcting certain defects of timbre common to many amateur singers, see suggestions on pages 78 to 81 regarding handling the voices.

After your choir has achieved the voice freedom made possible by this breathing, it will be easier to get the variety of tone color necessary for effective choral expression. As one writer says:

Contrasts of tone-color, contrasts of differently placed choirs, contrasts of sentiment, love, hate, hope, despair, joy, sorrow, brightness, gloom, pity, scorn, prayer, praise, exaltation, depression, laughter, tears—in fact all the emotions and passions are now expected to be delineated by the voice alone. It may be said, in passing, that in fulfilling these expectations choral singing has entered on a new lease of life.[5]

PHRASING

The director must learn how to indicate the thought that the composer expressed by his music and by the words. To determine the phrasing is not so difficult, as reading the words will usually make their meaning clear, and punctuation helps to set off the individual parts of the thought. In most cases

---

[5] Henry Coward, *Choral Technique and Interpretation* (London, 1914), p. 167.

each phrase should be sung with one breath, the breathing point coming at the end of the phrase. The good director will indicate this breathing place to his choir, and the singers will automatically phrase as he indicates. This is invaluable not only because all breathe at the right time, but also because they do not breathe at the wrong times. Thus they will phrase over all points the director desires to have connected.

There is a special phrasing beat which indicates to the choir that a break is to occur in the tone. This is made in the same manner as the beat which cuts off a hold; it is a beat that crosses the path of the other beats at a diagonal. It is usually made at the beginning of the beat on which the breath occurs and thus serves as a cutoff signal and also as a pickup and beat for the next note. In appearance the baton makes a gesture very much like a check mark; thus it is related to the cutoff beat in that it comes down to end the tone. But unlike the cutoff beat, which stays down, the phrasing beat rises again and swings into the rhythmic pattern, indicating that the tone is to be picked up and continued. There is no mistaking the phrasing beat even though it does not always go to a very low point. There is usually no need of having it go as low as the bottom point that beat one reached. An example of the phrasing beat is shown using the second measure of the hymn "Sun of My Soul" as an example:

Sun of my Soul , Thou Sav — ior. Dear

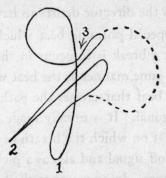

FIG. 14.—THE PHRASING BEAT

At the second beat of the second measure, instead of the baton's beating out beat two it rises and then makes the phrasing beat, arriving at the bottom of the stroke just at "two." The voices still having the word to complete will move to the note E at count two. Seeing the cutoff signal, they will immediately put on the final consonant to complete the word by about the end of half a beat. They will take a catch breath, and seeing that the baton has kept on moving they will be ready to sing "Thou" at the third beat. It is well to train the choir by occasionally omitting the phrasing beat in places like this during rehearsal and having them follow the directing by singing through the next phrase without a breath. It trains them to alertness.

The phrasing beat is also given at the end of a phrase ending with a half, a dotted half, or a whole note. In such cases the phrasing beat is made on the last beat before the entrance of the next note, in much the same manner as a hold would have been handled.

THE USE OF THE LEFT HAND IN DIRECTING

It is best to practice using the left hand to direct the beats, making the motions correspond with those of the right hand, except that the motion for the left hand in 3/4 time is down, left, up, instead of down, right, up, as it is for the right hand. Similarly in 4/4 time, the left hand moves down, right, left, up.

In actual directing the left hand should be used sparingly, since ordinarily this would be merely a duplicating of gesture when no duplication was necessary. Both hands may be used in this manner when extra emphasis is needed or when extra attention is wanted for a change of rhythm or volume. The use of the two hands will help hold the voices together through the change.

At other times it is better to use the left hand

chiefly as an extra expression indicator, to show when louder or softer passages are desired and how much change is wanted. It should help bring in one section or another of the choir at times when there is a new entrance to make while the rest of the choir continues to sing.

To indicate this kind of an entrance, the right hand continues beating time, while the left hand is poised ready to begin, much as it would be at the beginning of a composition. The director looks at the section which is to make the new entrance to see that every member is ready and to show them that it really is their section that should begin. Then one beat ahead of the entrance the left hand indicates a pickup beat, often moving slightly toward the entering group, again to indicate that it is their entrance. After the entrance has been made the left hand may continue to beat out the rhythm or it may let the right hand carry out that duty while the left indicates variations in expression or waits for a new entrance.

Chapter 4

DIRECTING WITHOUT A BATON

THE DIRECTIONS SO FAR GIVEN HAVE DEALT WITH the use of a baton. This is training every director should have whether he is going to use one or not. Now, however, the director should decide for himself whether he prefers to direct with a baton or to use the hands only. Having learned baton technique, it will be a simple matter to change and direct without the "stick." The chief point to decide is one's personal preference. To help clarify the matter, let us consider some of the disadvantages and advantages of dispensing with the baton.

There are three major disadvantages, part of them arising from misuse of the hands.

1. The greatest disadvantage is that too many directors forget baton technique when they do not use a baton. The gestures become merely up and down movements, or a smooth moving back and forth without enough definiteness to distinguish the beats; or else they become a fluttering type of movement that is humorous rather than inspiring.

2. Another disadvantage is that often the hand can

not be made to appear as graceful as if it assumed a definite position in grasping a baton.

3. The larger the chorus, the bigger the motions necessary in order that the singers will see them and will definitely feel the beat. The baton serving as an extension of the arm helps to make the motions visible without so much effort having to be expended.

On the other hand the advantages, especially considered from the point of view of a church choir director, are several.

1. Since the choir ordinarily is a small group and no member has difficulty in seeing the director, he does not need to make very large movements to enable the singers to follow him. Thus by use of the hands only, the gestures create less disturbance of the audience. Since a church choir should establish and maintain the feeling of worship, the more the attention is caught by the singing and the less by the mechanics, the better this worshipful attitude can be maintained.

2. A hand can be much more expressive than a stick. For any composition in which rhythm is the predominant feature, time beating (such as is done by a baton) is sufficient. But in a subjective composition full of deep feeling, the hand alone can much better indicate the modulations of voice and expression than can a baton.

3. The baton is an impersonal foil and partly takes

the personality away from the director. Directing by hand is much more personal; and since interpretation is largely dependent upon the individual judgment of the director, it is well for him to come into as close personal contact with his choir as is possible.

SUGGESTIONS

Now that the director has used a baton, he should go through many of the same exercises directing without the baton. Ordinarily, especially in beginning work, it will be well for the hand to follow the usual rhythmic pattern of beating time.

For a lyric (subjective) style of conducting, the hand (right) should be held relaxed, the fingers curved, and somewhat more open than when they are holding the baton. See Figure 15. The wrist should

Fig. 15.—Indicating Soft Tones When Directing
Without a Baton

be flexible. As when using the baton, the vigor and size of the first beat will indicate the strength of tone desired. If softening of the tone is desired, the hand can be opened up, palm downward, much as the left hand is used to indicate softening. This is most graceful if the fingers remain slightly curved. The straighter or stiffer the fingers are, the stronger the choir's responding tone.

For a dramatic (objective) style of conducting the fingers should straighten out more than they do for a lyric style and should be held almost rigid. The wrist will not be as flexible and the palm should turn at least slightly upward. With this style of directing the choir will respond with a stronger and firmer tone. A firm beat with fairly large swing will call out almost full volume from the choir. The means of softening and increasing the tone are the same as when directing a lyric tone, and the left hand will help in indicating variations in expression and in bringing in new entrances of various sections the same as when a baton is held in the right hand.

After experience has been gained, it will be found that it is often desirable to direct words and syllables rather than beats in a subjective number. In such case the rhythmic pattern is partially discarded although the down beat still represents "one"; for other syllables appearing on other beats, if they are indicated by a downward motion of the hand, the motion is partially sidewards, and the low point of the beat is higher than for "one." This type of directing leads to smoothness of phrasing, but care must be taken that the rhythmic feeling is not lost, since it is easy for it to become just a "down-up-down-up" type of directing with no feeling of where "one" is, or whether it is 3/4, 4/4, or 6/8 rhythm. That is one of the big dangers of directing without a baton. In objective compositions it is well to use the rhythmic pattern consistently, as rhythm is a predominant feature of these compositions. Nuances either in rhythm or volume occur seldom, and when they do occur they are on a broader scale than in subjective music. In the latter, nuances, mood changes, and subtle changes of expression are the order of the day, and the director is interpreting expression predominately rather than rhythm. In such cases the hands alone can draw from the choir far more response than a baton could do. I have seen directors of *a cappella* choirs lay aside their batons when they came to a composition of this type, even when they use one at other times. It must be that even they feel handicapped by having to hold on to a foil.

Last winter at a concert given by a nationally known *a cappella* choir, the director used a baton consistently for the first half of the program. Then he laid aside the baton while he directed a short subjective number, a Bach chorale, with the hands alone. The audience was held spellbound by the singing of the choir in this number. Several persons remarked afterwards that it was the best number of the program. They believed the director should have conducted without a baton all the time.

As you gain experience you will find your control over the choir becoming greater and greater. However, many little habits and personalities will creep into your directing. If they get results and are not disturbing to the choir or to the audience it is all right to keep them. But such habits as wiggling the eyebrows, beating time with the elbows, nodding the head, or bending the knees—and they creep in very easily—should be guarded against. Wiggling a finger to soften a singer or a section is permissible, as is limited facial expression (no contortions) to indicate pleasure or warning. If the director smiles when he is pleased, the members will try much harder to sing well than if he shows continually a "poker face."

Chapter 5

GENERAL CHOIR TECHNIQUE

NOT UNTIL THE DIRECTOR HAS ATTAINED A FACILITY of hand both for beating time and indicating expression is he ready to appear before his choir and really make the most of its possibilities.

General gestures of directing can be adapted to almost any group of singers; but when it comes to developing and improving a choir and getting the most out of it, every choir will be found to be different and to present problems of its own; and the ingenuity of the best trained director will be taxed. Suggestions are offered covering only a few cases. The student must draw what help he can from these, and thereafter test out his own ideas as his experience, reading, and imagination present them to him.

SELECTING THE VOICES

If the director inherits his choir from a previous administration he will not have much to say about the type he wants. In a small church group there is usually little enough choice, anyhow, since hard feelings can be created if volunteers are turned down. However, there are a few things it is well to know which will at least give a guide as to what type of new members to accept.

It will be found that a mixed group of very young and comparatively old people will not co-operate. Each group unconsciously resents the other; and where a choice is possible it is preferable to have the younger group. In the male section this matters very little; the older men are not resented either by the young men or by the girls, and they will nearly always co-operate well. Their voices usually retain a blending quality also; but in the women's section it is different. A greater change will be noticed in the maturing of the voice and in deterioration with the advancing of age. A voice that has been misused or abused will begin to deteriorate by thirty-five, or even earlier; and a strong voice, even one that has been well trained, begins to lose its blending quality by about forty. These figures may of course vary as much as ten years depending upon the voice and the type of use it has been given. These older voices gradually lose their flexibility and vitality. They will serve satisfactorily in a dramatic tone, but not so well in a lyric tone. Young voices (15-25) are lighter, more flexible, and better able to portray the various shades of emotion needed in subjective numbers. More voices are required to give a full-bodied tone when the voices are all young, but a bright quality can be ob-

tained that never can come from older voices. If any
doubt is felt on this score, just listen to any of the
a cappella choirs that are found in nearly every college of the land.

Since it is the higher notes that lose their vitality
first, often older voices can be used in the alto section;
however, many women have a prejudice against singing alto, and this prejudice would have to be overcome
first. It often helps to point out that the alto part
is as important as the soprano, and is absolutely necessary for the harmony; also that singing an alto part
will develop musicianship much more quickly than
singing a melody. To quote Schumann: "Sing in
choruses industriously, especially the middle voices.
This will make you a good reader, and intelligent as a
musician."

A satisfactory balance of voices in the women's section could be suggested as two-thirds young voices
(15-25) and one-third mature voices (25-35). This
will give the flexibility and lilt of youth and the rich-
ness of maturity, and will insure a full yet free quality
that neither youth nor maturity alone can give.

In selecting older singers refuse those persons whose
voices have been worn out in service or are radically
defective, and those who have sung for a long time
but never have learned to read music. These types
usually are incapable of improvement, yet unfortu-

nately they are the most faithful, and the hardest to get rid of once they have been admitted.

In testing voices for membership and in placing them in the right section remember that it is not range that determines whether a voice is soprano or alto, tenor or bass, but the voice quality or weight. A woman's low mellow voice would sing alto even though it could reach high C, and a light thin voice would be a soprano even though it could not reach F. If in doubt about a voice, place the person with a few altos and sopranos if a woman, and with tenors and basses if a man, and have them all sing, both together and separately, while you listen to the individual voices. By comparing you will know what classification to give. This is especially true with younger singers. If your choir is made up of girls of high school age, it may be well to classify them entirely by this method. Line up the girls, and while they sing an exercise or scale over and over at various pitches, place them in order according to the weight of the voice, the deepest voice on your right, going upward until the lightest voice is on your left. Then pick your lowest third for your alto section.

SEATING THE CHOIR

The seating arrangement of a choir depends to an extent upon the size of the sections, the strength of the voices, and the size and arrangement of the choir loft. It is seldom that an ideal situation is found, and the director will have to decide what will best fit into his situation.

As a rule, sopranos are much more numerous than altos. It is fortunate that usually four or five altos can create a balanced tone against ten or twelve sopranos, providing the soprano voices are not too loud. Ordinarily the girls should form two rows of the choir with the altos forming one end of the rows and the sopranos the other end. If the altos are weak, timid, or few in number try to get them on the end where the accompaniment is heard the most plainly. In the case of a piano or small organ this will be next to the instrument; but often in the case of a pipe organ, when the grille is quite high on the wall, they should be in the section farthest from the grille. If the choir is placed at an angle to the congregation, the weaker section should be nearest to the people as the voices will be that much more distinct. It is fairly customary to locate the altos on the right and the sopranos on the left (the directors right and left as he faces the choir); but when for any reason it seems advisable to reverse this position, there is no reason why it should not be done. Many amateur choirs have been placed with the altos seated behind the sopranos.   This arrangement is not recommended, for three reasons:

1. The director will not hear his alto tone as distinctly as when it is seated alongside of the soprano.

2. It seems to relegate the altos to a place of secondary importance, when really they are equally important with the sopranos.

3. The director will find it hard to indicate entrances and special features of expression to the altos, and will soon find himself directing for the sopranos alone, leaving the altos and the men to shift for themselves.

The customary and usually the most satisfactory seating arrangements for small church choirs are shown in the diagrams of Figure 16.

The proportions of a well-balanced choir in which no voice is unduly strong would be about ten sopranos to six altos, and five tenors to nine or ten basses. These are of course only general proportions which will vary according to the individual and combined strength of the voices and to the material available. Ordinarily one does not find enough of either basses or tenors.   Sometimes the proportion is far off.   I have found a choir which had twice as many tenors as true basses.   In such cases (for a volunteer choir) one doesn't dismiss unwanted voices, but tries to get

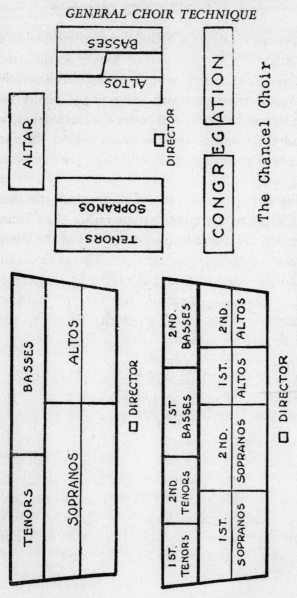

Fig. 16.—Choir Seating Plans

the sections to obtain a balanced tone by listening to each other as they sing, and by having sections that are too strong soften a little more. The relative position of the tenors and basses is not vitally important, but ordinarily it is better for the tenors to be behind the sopranos and the basses behind the altos as the high voices help each other and the low voices do likewise.

Where it is possible, it is wise to place the choir at an angle to the congregation rather than facing it directly. It should be considered part of the service and not an independent group. The choir should sing to the glory of God and not to bring glory on itself. When the singers do not face the audience directly but face the altar or the pulpit at least partially, the sentiment of both choir and congregation will be more worshipful.

The problem of seating individuals in the choir is a touchy one. If the director takes over a group that has functioned for a long time he may have to go slowly in making changes until he is certain of the temperament of his singers. For some reason or other most of the temperamental singers are in the soprano section, and this is the section that needs seating attention most, because it is here that the greatest variation of voices is found and here that unpleasant qualities are most noticeable.

If all voices in a section were the same in quality, then they could be seated according to height with the taller people in the second row. However, height will have to be a secondary consideration. Be sure the choir feels that the second row is as important as the first. Do not let the young and weak voices all sit in the second row. At least a few of the strongest voices should be there, and one or more good readers; for the second row can help the first row, but the first row gives little help to the second row. Another reason for putting stronger voices in back—voices which stand out because of their volume—is that a person in the second row will not sing as loudly as one in the front row, since those in front hear all the voices and will sing more freely, while those behind hear fewer voices and will as a consequence sing a little softer in order to be sure to blend. Here is another detail: if you have a singer who thinks she is a soloist and wants to be heard above the choir, put her in the back row and on the end. She will sing more softly here without realizing it, and at the same time will assist the rest of the section. This point of helping the others by her ability to read and carry the part might be played up as the reason for placing her there. On the other hand, the person you consider to be the best singer in point of tone quality, reading ability, and following a director should be placed as close to you as possible, in the front row and at the center of the choir. She will sing with the most confidence in this position and therefore will be of the most help to the choir.

BLENDING THE VOICES

Getting a good tone quality from the choir and getting the voices to blend usually is the hardest problem. A nasal penetrating voice or a hard flat quality can be very upsetting. Yet every choir director finds one or more voices of this kind.

The first step in developing the voices and in tone blending is to be sure the choir members are breathing diaphragmatically, or at least are making an attempt to do so. It will be well to type off copies of the explanation of diaphragmatic breathing given on page 56 and to give a copy to each member. Demonstrate breathing for them, explain it thoroughly, and give them a chance to try it. Ask them to study the explanation and to practice it at home; then occasionally take a couple of minutes of the rehearsal time for breathing exercises. The purpose of this is chiefly to keep breathing in their minds as one of the important features of singing.

To obtain soft blending tones have the choir sing in unison a song that does not run high. Almost any solo part of an anthem will do, for example, "Blessed

Redeemer" (pages 93-96), or a hymn such as "Softly and Tenderly Jesus Is Calling." First have the choir hum the melody. Tell the members to note as they hum that they cannot pick out individual voices. All the voices will seem to blend into one tone. Then have them sing the melody softly on the vowel o͞o trying to make the voices blend as perfectly as they did when humming. Again have them sing the melody on the same vowel, but making their voices sound as deep as possible (this can be done by dropping the jaw more while the lips still retain their o͞o shape); now have them sing the words very softly while they still keep their mouths as near this deep o͞o shape as they can. It will be noticed that the long e and short i sounds are mellowed to a sound very like the German umlaut *u* (*ü*), and the long *a* and short *e* sound are mellowed to a sound very much like the German umlaut *a* (*ä*). These sounds when produced in this way are very much softer than the thinner *e* or *a* sounds can be made. This tone deepening is of use in making the effect mellow and in developing easier control. It should be used only in very soft singing, although it may be well for the sopranos to mellow their brighter vowel sounds (long *e* and *a*, and short *e* and *i*) in this manner whether they are soft or loud, for a much better blending of tone will result. Care must be taken that this is not overdone, of course.

A penetrating, pointed voice or a twangy quality of voice can be somewhat mellowed and improved by using this type of tone production.

To demonstrate what really soft singing is, place a loud-ticking alarm clock at some distance from the choir and have them sing in the above manner but so softly that they can still hear the ticking of the clock. They will be surprised that this is possible, and you will get results that will delight you.

High tones can be helped immensely just by an improvement in breathing. They will often be further helped by opening the mouth sufficiently wide.

The more plainly the breath support can be felt at the diaphragm, the firmer the tone will be. Have the singers place a hand over the diaphragm and then sing a series of low notes followed by high ones (octaves) using the vowel sound ah. Tell them to sing with full voice and keep the expansion at the diaphragm as they sing the higher notes as well as on the lower notes. When this is done it will be found that the tone is full, comparatively free, and feels easy to sing. Have them practice this a number of times and promise to do it at home. Also ask them to sing the exercise alternately loudly and softly, for singing it softly makes a further development in the vocal muscles. Very shortly the voices will be much improved, and the choir will be able to sing high notes both softly and loudly without discomfort or fear.

Too often the altos sound like sopranos and the basses sound like high baritones. To develop a full alto tone and a full deep bass tone, have these sections practice their parts of an anthem, deepening their voices as much as possible—using diaphragmatic breathing—and getting the mouth to feel much as though they were beginning to yawn. A prompt change will be noticed in the depth and quality of the tone. This exercise need not be persisted in very long, for soon their throats will relax and open up naturally and a deep tone will result without conscious effort. Care must be taken that the tones do not become throaty. They should remain just as clear as they were originally, but deeper in quality. *Ah* must remain *ah* and not become *aw*. Also watch that the basses do not pull back their chins when they try to sing low notes.

REHEARSALS

1. Never undervalue hymns as a means of choir development either in a rehearsal or as a special number for Sunday service. A well-sung hymn makes a suitable special number at any time. It would be wise if beginning choirs used more noble hymns in-

stead of some of the uninspired easy anthems to be found on the market.

When hymns are rehearsed, care must be taken that they are phrased according to the thought expressed, and not every two measures, as so often is done. Be sure they are sung with feeling and expression. Inspire love for good hymns by speaking of them with respect and giving them as much consideration as you give to an anthem.

2. Lay your plan ahead of time as to how the rehearsal is to be spent, what numbers are to be rehearsed, and their approximate order. Begin with a number that is well known and singable. An objective number will be better than a subjective number for this purpose; this will open up the voices and give a feeling of freedom and joy in singing. To begin with an unknown number means stumbling and stopping and is altogether a disheartening beginning for all concerned. If a successful beginning has been made, new and difficult things will be undertaken with much more enthusiasm. Close with a well-known number also. The singers like to relax and really sing; if they do this just before they go home, the rehearsal will leave a pleasant memory that will bring them back to the next rehearsal. Do not spend most of the time on one number. Six or eight numbers should be run through at every rehearsal, including

two well-know numbers, one or two new ones, and two or three that are in the process of development. Spend several weeks on a number before it is performed in public.

3. Do not make it a practice to have certain sections drill on their parts while the other sections are silent. The waiting singers are wasting time, talking, and becoming restless, while the section practicing is learning by rote instead of by note. True, hard places may have to be run through section by section, but take only the hard places, and do not spend much time on one section. Keep every one busy. If longer section rehearsals are necessary on a difficult number, then if possible send these sections to various rooms or to near-by homes where there are pianos and let them practice there during a certain allotted time. After this they should return for ensemble rehearsal. By this, all have been kept busy and those who need it have had a chance for individual practice.

If most numbers are learned without section rehearsals, gradually the members will learn to read their parts and to become self-sufficient. Continued part practice makes the members more and more dependent and afraid to try anything new until they have learned it by rote.

4. Begin punctually. Beginning late is a vice that grows upon a membership unless it is checked im-

mediately. If the full choir has not arrived by scheduled starting time, begin with what you have so that their time is not wasted. This will tend to speed up the latecomers into arriving punctually.

5. Do not make the rehearsal too long. An hour and a half of singing with no wasted time is all most voices can stand. A great deal can be accomplished in an hour and a half if you work industriously. Your singers will appreciate knowing what time they can plan to leave, and that you will stay by the time set.

6. Give encouragement and praise generously.

7. Keep everybody busy! Give no time for inattention to creep in. The most important item of the rehearsal: "Keep everybody busy."

8. It is wise at times to give a few special drills in following a conductor's beat, in making smooth crescendos and diminuendos, and in enunciation. Exercise of this type should be given on one pitch or on a very familiar melody so that the singers can concentrate on the drill rather than on the notes. In such exercises the director should introduce unexpected holds, breath marks, accelerandos, ritards, and accents. In drilling the choir to make crescendos and diminuendos, be sure these are smooth like this

and not spurts like this.

In singing several words during a crescendo be sure
it occurs on the words rather than between the words,
not merely with each word sung louder than the previous one.

PROGRAMING AND PERFORMANCES

1. Try as far as possible to fit the anthem or special number to the service. If the musical numbers
are based on the text or the scripture reading, the
lesson is driven home with double force. Where this
is not possible, at least have the special number har-
monize with the service in spirit.

2. The singers should be decorous during the service. Whispering between numbers must not be al-
lowed. Choir members have a greater obligation to
the church than merely singing special music; they
must be in sympathy with what the church stands
for and in harmony with the service. This in itself
should prevent whispering and levity; but if any
forget themselves, they must be reminded of their
obligation to the service. Usually a word in private
will be enough, for most of this type of disturbance
comes from thoughtlessness rather than from inten-
tion. Often a look or a shake of the head will quiet

an offender if his or her eye can be caught at the right time.

2. In a special program seek to give variety. Combine both choral numbers and solos, alternating them when possible. When two choral numbers are used in succession, be sure to use different types, that is, numbers with contrasting moods, and if possible written in different keys. A slow number should be followed by a fast one, or vice versa, and a dramatic one by a subjective number. Do not have two soloists with the same type of voice sing successively, such as two sopranos, or a soprano and a tenor. Secure as much contrast as possible without destroying the mood of the concert. Do not mix sacred and secular numbers. If secular numbers are to be used, place them in a separate part of the program.

4. Drill the choir members on standing and being seated together. A slight motion of the hands should be enough of a signal for rising, and a slight, slow nod enough for being seated. They should rise and be seated comparatively slowly. In this way it will be easier to make the action uniform.

5. A program should not last longer than an hour. It is better for an audience to go home feeling that it was too short, rather than worn out or thinking it was too long to sit still.

A CAPPELLA SINGING

Singing without accompaniment is the most effective singing a choir can do. Any choir that doesn't do some of this type has missed an experience. Besides this, it gives the best kind of all-around development. Some *a cappella* work should be done at every rehearsal. It develops keenness of harmonic feeling, purity of intonation, ensemble quality and balance, and also appreciation of choral singing. Anything that does all this must not be neglected. Even numbers that are to be sung with accompaniment can well be rehearsed at times without the accompaniment. The organ can "cover a multitude of sins" which will not be discovered until it is silent. If the number can be sung well without accompaniment, it will be sung well with it.

It is good policy to practice hymns *a cappella* before regular anthems are attempted. Hymns have an easy four-part harmony with which the singers will be familiar. But make the choir sing more expressively than it would if it sang with accompaniment.

Watch the voices carefully to guard against flatting, sharping, or faulty intonation. All sections must be watched on high notes, or upward skips, especially of a fourth, or ascending or descending scale and chromatic passages, the ends of phrases, and sustained tones. Correcting faults in such places will be done more by thinking than by mere practicing. Find the faulty spot and teach the choir to sing it while thinking it high enough; thus the mind will be trained to know what to do in other similar places.

Instruct the singers to listen to all the sections at the same time that they are singing. That is necessary if purity of intonation is to be maintained between the parts. Any time a chord is sung that does not sound well, the choir should be stopped and made to hold the chord and listen to it in its pure form.

THE ACCOMPANIST

Fortunate is the director who has a good accompanist, for she can almost make or break the choir. A singer who has the necessary organ technique will ordinarily make a better accompanist than a non-singing organist.

The accompanist is second to the director, and must understand that the director is the interpreter of the music. On the other hand, there must be the most cordial relationship between the two, or difficulties will constantly arise. Much of the responsibility for the relationship between director and accompanist rests upon the director. It is unnecessary to say that he must treat her with courtesy and respect and fairness. Her responsibility in a way is greater than his own, for she must play the entire service as well as the special choir numbers. She must be at all rehearsals and perhaps at other services during the week. If at times she becomes "difficult," the director must keep these facts in mind, for she may be merely tired.

The director must guard against letting the organist "lead" him. If he is not sure of his tempo, she will naturally set her own. Sometimes unless the director is insistent, the organist will choose her own tempo and interpretation in spite of the director.

If the organist is dependable and a good musician, it is a courtesy to let her play the introduction of special numbers without beating time for her. A nod from the director should be sufficient to let her know that everything is ready and that she may begin to play; and he should not beat time until he begins with the choir. In the case of an orchestral introduction the situation is different.

If the accompanist is a poor sight reader, then in fairness to her and to yourself give her the music so that she has plenty of time to prepare it in advance of the rehearsal.

AN EXAMPLE OF HOW TO STUDY AN ANTHEM

Blessed Redeemer (pages 93-96) is one of the best anthems that can be found for beginning instruction or for developing tone quality and expression in a choir. Its range is medium; no note is difficult to reach; it has an appealing melody; and it is capable of a great variety of expression.

The stanza should be sung by the women, being studied and sung first in the manner suggested on pages 78 and 79 under the heading "Blending the Voices." In both rehearsal and performance it should be sung with this soft mellow tone with the brighter vowels modified as was previously suggested. The chorus, being objective in nature, should be sung with a dramatic tone, that is, a louder and more open quality.

The introduction should be played at about a tempo of $\text{♩}= 68$. The starting tone should be moderately loud and of a joyous quality. At measure 6 a diminuendo begins, and at measure 7 a strong ritard is made. Measure 8 is played in tempo again, leading directly into the voice entrance, softly, but with no hesitation. This part of the stanza may be sung by all the sopranos and altos with the type of tone suggested above. Be sure the tone is broken momentarily after "Redeemer," measure 10, in order to set the words "Blessed Redeemer" off from the rest of the phrase and make them a title of address, a title of love.

Begin a slight crescendo at measure 13, continuing this to the beginning of measure 16, where a diminuendo occurs while a strong ritard is made. Measure

17 begins in tempo again with the same soft tone as at the beginning. Be sure measures 13-16 and measures 17-20 are phrased over in one breath each.

Measure 21 should begin a little louder. A breath should be taken in the middle of measure 22 after "trouble," and from there to the end of measure 24 the tone should be softer and slower. A slight nuance should be made on each note of measure 23, that is, a slight pulsation that starts softly, and makes a crescendo and a diminuendo on each note. This can be indicated by a mark over the notes.

The altos sing measures 25-28 alone, singing softly and in strict tempo. A slight crescendo should be made on the triplet figures at the end of measures 25 and 26. Each note of all the triplet figures should be sung in a clean-cut manner. In practice the notes might be sung at first as though the word were ha-ha-hand (using measure 25 as an example). Then sing the notes just as distinctly but without any "h" appearing in the tone.

At measure 29 the sopranos use a little stronger tone, but apply the same crescendos over all three sets of triplets, making the notes clean-cut and distinct and with a slight ritard on the phrase "to see."

The altos and sopranos sing the duet measures 33-36. The first part should be very soft with a nuance on the words "the blessings" and a ritard with a crescendo should be used on the words "my days."

All voices enter measure 37 with a strong, clear tone—about a tempo of ♩ = 56. A crescendo should continue to measure 40, which should be held. Measure 41 begins loud and in the faster tempo, and the singing remains strong till measure 43 where a diminuendo begins. The last note of measure 46 and on through measure 48 are sung softly and with a ritard. Measure 48 is sung with a hold.

Measure 49 begins the same as measure 41. The tone remains strong to measure 53 where a diminuendo begins. The last note of measure 54 and on to the end should be sung moderately loud and slower, with the same pulsation of tone in measure 55 that was explained for measure 23. The first time the chorus is sung, "be Thine evermore" is one smooth phrase; the second time it should be slower, making a hold on "Thine," and taking a breath before finishing "evermore," slowly. The second stanza should be sung in the same manner as the first, with the full introduction being played.

Blessed Redeemer

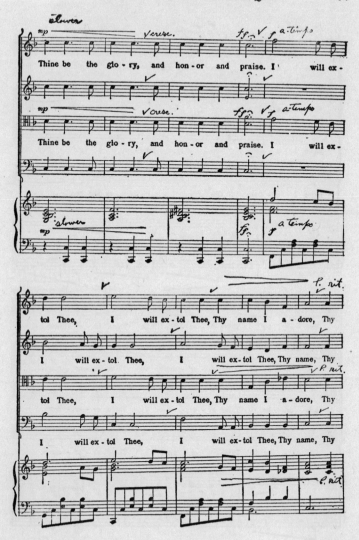

Chapter 6

THE SINGER-DIRECTOR AND THE
ORGANIST-DIRECTOR

THE SINGER-DIRECTOR AND THE ORGANIST-DIRECTOR
have a handicap in securing the best development and
results from a choir because their attention is divided
between the work of the choir and their own special
work of either playing or singing. Furthermore,
there is not the personal control and direction that
gives surety to the attacks and releases and control to
the variations in expression.

However, in spite of these difficulties it is possible
for such a director to accomplish much with his
choir if he will prepare the music fully in advance
of rehearsal and is in a position to help control the
singers by sight, rather than by sound alone.

The music should be gone over in advance of choir
rehearsal and given all marks possible. The expression desired and all breath marks should be indicated,
as well as the tone wanted, together with any special
effects that might otherwise be forgotten. The
anthem "Blessed Redeemer" on the preceding pages
is marked in this manner and will serve as an example
of such advance marking.

To save time and labor, some of the copies should have the marks placed only over the soprano line, some only over the alto, some only over the tenor, and the rest only over the bass. The proper designation should be written on the front of each copy, and when the sheets are handed out, each section will receive its own specially marked copies. Without such marks the choir will make very little variation in its expression, since no director is before it to concentrate attention on these things; and if the music is marked after the rehearsal instead of before, a certain value of familiarity is lost. Having the choir members mark the music during the rehearsal, while it has the value of concentrating their thoughts on these variations of expression, will soon become monotonous and lose time that could better be used in singing. Also, since the marks will be made by many persons, some will be made poorly or will be illegible, and thus are even worse than valueless.

Both types of director should spend a great deal of the rehearsal time standing before the group and directing with gestures. For the organist-director this will mean *a cappella* singing unless there is an assistant who can play during this period. The last few times a number is sung in its final preparation should be under circumstances similar to those under which it will be sung in public. The value of standing before his group lies in the far greater control over the singers. Much less time will be lost in stopping the choir to say that some particular place must be sung softer, that the nuance must be greater, or other like comments. A director using hand gestures can bring about satisfactory results with much less stopping and talking than can anyone else. After the choir has sung a number properly a few times it can more safely be depended upon to continue in that manner. Of course the director, even though standing before his group, should follow the expression marks every time exactly as he has placed them on the music. This is an advantage that the man who stands before his group also in performance has over others. With responsive singers he can vary the expression as the inspiration of the moment moves him.

The organist-director often thinks he can control his choir entirely by the way he plays the accompaniments. This is true to an extent, but nearly always it results in the choir's following the organ instead of being with the organ. The organist should be seated in such a manner that he can see most of the choir members and be seen by them if this control is to be anywhere nearly complete. A nod of the head to indicate an attack or a release, and a slight motion of the lifted hand to bring about a softer or louder tone helps immeasurably, both in the quality of the resultant tone and in the confidence with which the choir proceeds. Care must be taken that motions are not overdone and do not attract attention from the audience, and that in trying to keep gestures inconspicuous, facial expressions are not magnified until they become facial contortions.

The singer-director must be seen by all of his or her choir membership or one of two things will result: either the organist becomes the one whom the choir follows, or the singer leads out with his voice until the other singers hear and merely follow. If this happens, the audience hears the voice also, and the result is a solo voice with choir accompaniment. For the best results the singer-director either must stand in the front row with all the other singers turning slightly toward him or her—and be in full view of the organist—or a large mirror must be placed across from the choir in which the members can see the director. In this way he can direct by slight nods of the head such points as attacks and releases and ritards. Again, these signs must be very inconspicuous, or the attention of the audience will be centered on watching the nods rather than on the singing. It might be said that if the organist can see the director she will follow him and then the choir will follow her. However, in such a case it really becomes a following instead of what it should be, a singing with the director. One very large church in Chicago has a well-known bass singer and teacher for its director. He directs from his position in the bass section by using marked copies and a mirror. His choir secures remarkable *a cappella* results. The singers are seated in the chancel with the sopranos and tenors facing the altos and basses. The sopranos and tenors can see the director since he is opposite them. Above and behind the tenors a large mirror hangs in which the altos and basses, on the opposite side, watch the director.

Other schemes might be worked out under other circumstances. Remember that only when the director is seen can he hold his choir together to a uniformity of attack and expression.

Chapter 7

RECOMMENDED ANTHEMS FOR A VOLUNTEER CHOIR

IN SELECTING ANTHEMS FOR HIS CHOIR, THE DIREC-
tor must remember to include only those which make
a genuine musical appeal. Each number must be
studied individually, and this question should be
asked: "Was this anthem composed by inspiration or
only by labor of mind?" In other words, was it
written because the text created a musical idea that
must express itself, or was it written only because
there was a chance to sell a new anthem? Never be
satisfied with an inferior anthem because the choir
must have easy music. It would be better to sing
less often and perform only good music, or to repeat
numbers more often, than to sing "hack writing"
because the choir can't afford better music or hasn't
had time to learn something better.

A LIST OF EASY ANTHEMS FOR A BEGINNING CHOIR

The anthems recommended here are all very easy,
but they are thoroughly musical and require a variety
of expression for effective interpretation. They will
create musical development in a beginning choir, yet

they are worthy of performance by any choir no matter what its state of development.

Ambrose—ONE SWEETLY SOLEMN THOUGHT. A choir arrangement of the well-known solo.

Andrus—THE LORD'S PRAYER. An easy but attractive *a cappella* arrangement of this prayer.

Arensky—THE LORD HATH HEARD ME. A number that is most effective when sung *a cappella*. It is short but is filled with beautiful tone colors and nuances.

Bach—Any of Bach's chorales are beautiful and should if possible be sung *a cappella*. Chorale collections may be bought. The following chorales are easy but melodious: BREAK FORTH, O BEAUTEOUS HEAVENLY LIGHT; IF THOU BUT SUFFER GOD TO GUIDE THEE; NOW LET ALL THE HEAVENS ADORE THEE.

Barnby—O LORD, HOW MANIFOLD. A jubilant harvest festival number.

Barnby—SWEET IS THY MERCY, LORD. A beautiful melody. It has a soprano solo with chorus accompaniment.

Denza-Fearis—BLESSED REDEEMER. This anthem is shown on pages 93-96.

Eastham—GLORY TO GOD IN THE HIGHEST. An excellent Christmas anthem.

Farrant—LORD, FOR THY TENDER MERCIES' SAKE. A slow, stately chorale.

Field—GOD SHALL WIPE AWAY ALL TEARS. An interesting anthem that lies low for both sopranos and tenors.

Gaul—REJOICE IN THE LORD ALWAYS. An anthem of praise that permits more interpretative feeling than most.

Gaul—THIS IS THE DAY. A spirited number suitable for any special celebration.

Harker—TURN YE EVEN TO ME. This is largely written in unison, but it is very interesting and maintains good attention.

Haydn—SEE HIM! SEE HOW THE RIGHTEOUS ONE DIETH. A motet for the Passion Season. Very moving. Should be *a cappella*.

Himmel—INCLINE THINE EAR. An attractive melody written in the hymn-anthem style.

Hopkins—LIFT UP YOUR HEADS. A stately number that may be used either for Palm Sunday or as a general anthem of praise.

Huerter—RISE UP, MY SOUL, AND STRETCH THY WINGS. A short but spirited setting for this well-known hymn.

Maker—AWAKE, THOU THAT SLEEPEST. An Easter anthem that is inspiring. It goes to G, but is otherwise easy.

Maker—PRAISE THE LORD. A splendid number for either harvest festival or general use.

Moore—INVOCATION. A very pleasing number that may be used either as an invocation or a general anthem.

Mozart—JESU, WORD OF GOD INCARNATE. An excellent communion number, especially when used *a cappella*.

Negro spirituals—Several spirituals that can be found in community songbooks are suitable for church use. Among them are: STEAL AWAY, which can be made very worshipful and appealing; WERE YOU THERE? which is suitable for any occasion around Easter.

Netherlands Folk Song—PRAYER OF THANKSGIVING. A well-known Thanksgiving melody suitable in any arrangement.

Nevin, George—He has written and arranged a number of hymn-anthems both from well-known and original melodies. One of the best of the latter is JESUS, MY SAVIOR, LOOK ON ME. Two solo stanzas and two chorus stanzas which are effective when sung *a cappella*.

Novello—LIKE AS A HART. There is a repetition of phrases, but they are effective if made contrasting.

Ouseley—FROM THE RISING OF THE SUN. An excellent anthem especially for a mission Sunday or Epiphany.

Praetorius—Lo, How a Rose E'er Blooming. A beautiful Christmas number. Best when *a cappella*.

Schultz,—A Prayer for the New Year. A simple but very attractive New Year's anthem.

Scott—Supplication. A short anthem. It is especially effective when used as a prayer, invocation, or benediction.

Sibelius—O Morn of Beauty. A chorale from *Finlandia*. Exquisite tonal effects. Suitable for Easter or general use.

Simper—He has written several easy and medium-easy anthems. Among them are these: Break Forth Into Joy, an outstanding anthem for use either at Christmas or Easter; He Shall Reign Forever, a number containing excellent contrasts, suitable for Easter, Christmas, or special occasions; Make a Joyful Noise, a joyous anthem for general use or for special celebrations; The Lord is My Strength, a splendid anthem of praise suitable for general use.

Sullivan—Saviour, Thy Children Keep. An evening anthem that is much more interesting than most.

Tschaikowsky—The Lord's Prayer. Another easy but inspiring setting of this prayer.

Williams—THOU WILT KEEP HIM IN PERFECT PEACE. A very attractive anthem. Best when done *a cappella.*

Woodward—REJOICE GREATLY. An inspiring anthem for the advent season or for general use.

Wooler—BE THOU MY GUIDE. Another hymn-anthem that expresses deep feeling and is very much worth while.

Wooler—GIVE ME A PERFECT HEART, O LORD. A melodious hymn-anthem that is simple but very effective.

A LIST OF SLIGHTLY MORE DIFFICULT ANTHEMS

The following anthems are more difficult than those of the previous list but no number listed is too difficult for the average experienced amateur choir. Very few numbers contain more than four voice parts, and in any such cases the extra voices are called for only in short sections; no number contains rapid involved contrapuntal sections; and in nearly all the numbers the highest note required of the sopranos is F or G. Few anthems with longer solo passages are listed, since the object has been to select music that is essentially choral. To make the list still more useful, music is classified into two grades, the moderately easy and the moderately difficult—indicated by the letters E or M.

Atwood—Teach Me, O Lord. (E). A stately and pleasing anthem. The higest note is F.

Bach—Jesu, Priceless Treasure. First part (E), second part (M). A motet of three parts, each part harmonized differently. One of the most beautiful of Bach's chorales.

Barnby—Break Forth into Joy. (M). A jubilant Easter number. Needs good volume. Not difficult but has a few G's.

Beethoven—The Glory of God in Nature. (E). A majestic number that almost sings itself but requires volume. One G.

Blumenshein—My Soul Doth Magnify the Lord. (E). A number with excellent contrasts. Spirited movement. Highest note F.

Bortniansky—Cherubim Song No. 7. (E). Beautiful nuances and progressions. Short three-part section for women. Only one G.

Candlyn—Fierce Raged the Tempest. (M). Splendid chord effects and tonal contrasts. Several G's and one optional A.

Chenoweth—Hail to the King Victorious. (E). A martial processional anthem. Repetition of theme. One G (last note).

Christiansen—He has arranged many choir numbers. However, many are written for eight voices and are too hard for the average choir. He is one of the best choral writers of this country and nearly all his numbers are worth doing. Only a few can be named here: O BREAD OF LIFE (M), a beautiful number for communion or general use, having a baritone solo with women's chorus accompaniment, no high notes; O SACRED HEAD (M), especially for Good Friday—more than four parts, but can be handled easily.

Coleridge-Taylor—LIFT UP YOUR HEADS. (E). An excellent festival anthem. Short but inspiring. Has two G's.

Elgar—AS TORRENTS IN SUMMER. (M). An excellent *a cappella* number. Good for special programs. Highest note F.

Gadsby—O LORD, OUR GOVERNOR. (M). A fine "praise" number. Requires a good-sized chorus for volume. Several G's.

Goss—O SAVIOUR OF THE WORLD. (E). A fine anthem for use at communion or general services. Highest note F.

Goss—O TASTE AND SEE. (E). An attractive number that can be used on many occasions. Highest note is F.

Gounod—PRAISE YE THE FATHER. (E) A well-known objective "praise" anthem that never grows old. One high A.

Gounod—Send Out Thy Light. (E). A good number for any occasion. Long, but part may be omitted. Highest note G.

Grieg—Behold a Host. (E). Effective on All Saints' Day. Has a low solo with chorus accompaniment. No high notes.

Hamblen—He writes very melodious solos which have been arranged also for chorus. One of the best of these is Beside Still Waters. (E). Good for Shepherd Sunday or general use. Highest note F (optional A).

Handel—Holy Art Thou. (M). An arrangement of his famous "Largo." Needs a good-sized chorus. Several G's.

Hiles—Blessed Are the Merciful. (E). A very pleasing number based on the Beatitudes. Highest note is G.

Ivanoff—Bless the Lord, O My Soul. (E). Capable of very effective interpretation effects. Highest note is E.

Ivanoff—Incline Thine Ear. (M). An outstanding number, but it has a few difficult measures. Highest note is F sharp.

Ivanoff—Praise the Name of the Lord. (E). An attractive and showy number that is not hard except for a few G's.

Jones—BLESSED ARE THE PURE IN HEART. (M). An outstanding anthem based on the Beatitudes. Highest note is G.

Kopyloff—GOD IS A SPIRIT. (M). A splendid anthem that should be done *a cappella*. Highest note is F sharp.

MacFarlane—OPEN OUR EYES. (M). Exquisite chords. Worth any amount of work needed for preparation. Several G's.

Molitor—PRAISE YE THE LORD. (M). Rather showy without being difficult. Interesting to sing. Highest note F sharp.

Mozart—GLORIA from the *Twelfth Mass*. (M). Lies high for the sopranos but should be learned, if possible. Inspires joyousness and volume. Many G's.

Neidlinger—THE SILENT SEA. (M). Requires a soprano solo with the choir. Lovely effects. Solo goes to A flat.

Nevin—DEAR JESUS, SWEET THE TEARS I SHED. (E). A pleasing anthem of penitence. Highest note E.

Noble—He has several excellent arrangements. They are nearly all rather difficult. Both the following have a divided bass part and go to G: FIERCE WAS THE WILD BILLOW. (M), an outstanding anthem with good effects; SOULS OF THE RIGHTEOUS (M), a very good number for All Saints' Day and other memorial days.

Pike—ALL GLORY, LAUD AND HONOR. (E). A good praise anthem demanding a variety of tone. Highest note F.

Protheroe—THE NINETY AND NINE. (M). A somewhat difficult but attractive setting for this text. One G.

Randegger—PRAISE THE LORD. (M). Somewhat difficult but too good to leave out. Requires a couple of A's.

Rheinberger—NEAR IS THE LORD. (E). A very attractive *a cappella* number. Goes to G.

Roberts—PEACE I LEAVE WITH YOU. (E). A difficult tenor solo at the first. Chorus part is easy. Highest soprano note F.

Roberts—SEEK YE THE LORD. (E). Tenor solo at the first requires a pleasing voice. Chorus accompaniment not hard.

Rogers—GIVE THANKS UNTO THE LORD. (E). An attractive spirited anthem. Highest note is F.

Saint-Saens—PRAISE YE THE LORD. (M). From the *Christmas Oratorio*. Somewhat difficult but excellent. Goes to G.

Schuler—MY DEFENSE IS OF GOD. (E). An excellent spirited number all choirs should sing. Goes to F sharp.

Speaks—MORE LOVE TO THEE, O CHRIST. (E). A very appealing hymn-anthem. Good melodic progressions. Goes to F sharp.

Stainer—He has a large number of outstanding anthems that can be given by the average choir. All his works are excellent, particularly the following: FLING WIDE THE GATES (M), an outstanding number for Palm Sunday which goes to G; GOD SO LOVED THE WORLD (E) a number from "The Crucifixion" which every choir should have—it goes to G; THEY HAVE TAKEN AWAY MY LORD (E), an outstanding anthem for Easter which goes to F sharp; YE SHALL DWELL IN THE LAND (E), a good anthem for harvest festivals or general use which goes to F sharp.

Sullivan—I WILL SING OF THY POWER. (E). A spirited praise anthem. Has a pleasing tenor or soprano solo. Goes to F sharp.

Sullivan—TO THEE WE PRAY. (E). An attractive *a cappella* anthem. Goes to G.

Tschaikowsky—He has several outstanding anthems, but they are rather difficult. Two of the best numbers: FOREVER WORTHY IS THE LAMB (M), which has beautiful nuances and tonal effects and goes to A; A LEGEND (E), an outstandingly beautiful number for Passion Week or general programs, with only one G.

Turner—SUN OF MY SOUL. (E). An attractive evening hymn. Capable of excellent interpretation. Goes to G.

Watson—UNTO THEE, O GOD, DO WE GIVE THANKS. (E). A joyous Thanksgiving or Harvest Festival anthem. Goes to G.

West—THE LORD IS EXALTED. (M). A spirited number that will appeal. Goes only to F.

Woodward—THE DAY THOU GAVEST, LORD, IS ENDED. (M). An excellent evening anthem. Has one A.

Woodward—THE RADIANT MORN HATH PASSED AWAY. (E). A number that builds up to a splendid climax. Several G's.

Woodward—THE SUN SHALL BE NO MORE THY LIGHT. (E). A good anthem for general or Saints' Day use. Goes only to F.

Zingarelli—GO NOT FAR FROM ME, O GOD. (E). A very beautiful anthem. Begins subdued but ends joyously. Goes to G.

This list of anthems does no more than tap the field of good music. There are hundreds of other numbers that could be added. However, the list has attemped to introduce a number of composers of all periods and to present a variety of texts and treatments suitable for almost any occasion. Furthermore, it has selected these anthems from the catalogs of many publishers.

If this suggested list will only tend to establish the love for better music, then it has done its duty well; and the amateur director can then safely trust his own judgment in adding to the list.

Chapter 8

FINAL SUGGESTIONS

HERE ARE SOME FINAL SUGGESTIONS OFFERED WITH the hope that they may help earnest choir directors.

1. Do not sing with the choir during rehearsals. If the director sings with the sopranos they will become dependent and will listen for his voice instead of training themselves to independence in reading the notes. By singing any part the director cuts down his listening ability and does not really hear how the choir sounds. It is all right to help a weak section at times both in rehearsal and in performance, but it should be done very seldom. Whenever the director sings with the choir he should be sure that his voice blends. It is no better for the director's voice than for any other to sound out above the choir.

2. In most amateur choirs the solo parts of anthems should be sung by an entire section rather than by one voice unless there is an outstanding soloist who can sing without hurting the feelings of the other members. Solos will ordinarily sound better when sung by the entire section, since few choirs have members who can sing effectively alone. Furthermore, a solo passage can thus be used as training for

several people. This use of entire sections cuts down the personality feature and the music becomes more worshipful. Also no comments can be made afterwards, such as, "Someone else could have sung it better," or "He always gives her the solos." Of course an outstanding voice should be used when one is available; but often it is better to use such a voice in a complete solo number rather than in a short incidental solo. One must recognize exceptions in anthems which have distinctly solo parts.

3. When the soprano section is weak and does not reach its high notes with ease or fails to give them pleasing tone quality, it is often possible to sing a lower note in the chord that can be reached more easily, and still not spoil the melodic line. High notes do have a climatic and dramatic effect, but if they are not musical sounds the result is less pleasing than if lower notes were sung instead. Do not make this a habit, but use the lower notes only while the choir is gaining confidence. Any soprano section with a little training, even when it numbers only four or five, should be able to sing a G that is fairly full and pleasing. However, many small choirs with untrained voices are unable to reach an A with confidence. In such cases there is good reason for changing the note. This will make it possible to use certain numbers that otherwise might have to be omitted.

4. The choir should sing with confidence. If any members hesitate at some point because they are waiting for someone else to enter first, that point will be weak. Teach all to sing boldly even at the risk of making an error. It is easy to overlook errors made by one who is doing his best, for he has proved his good intentions and he will be capable of improvement. But one who continually hesitates does not help at any time, and he can never improve as long as he has that grave fault.

5. In training a choir, various details must be evaluated, as all cannot be equally emphasized. In this evaluation the thought that is to be expressed or the mood that is to be established must always take precedence over all else. Thus, if one were to divide the singing of a number into its three component parts—the words, the tone, and the notes—the relative value of these divisions would usually stand in that order. If the congregation does not understand the words, then it has missed the lesson. This means that the choir must make its words understood even if one of the other points must be sacrificed. Accuracy of notation alone cannot inspire, but clear words sung with real sincerity can do so even when errors are made such as lack of voice blending or some slight inaccuracy of pitch.

From the start of his work the director must stress

the singing of words understandably. His first drilling must be in pronunciation and enunciation. The learning of new songs and drilling in purity of intonation can be continued as the choir progresses, but the clarity of the words should be demanded from the first.

To establish the habit of singing the words clearly —and that includes singing them expressively—new pieces should be sung in entirety at the first rehearsal so that the choir members themselves know the message. The director may have to emphasize certain phrases by explanation as well as by indicating expression, but his goal should be to have his choir feel the sentiments which they are singing. At first in studying a number the notes are the least important part. They can be learned after the emotional content is established. Thinking first of notes often means that they are the main thing thought of during the performance. Notes can be made of secondary importance and still be sung accurately.

In the study of words remember that it is the vowels that are sung while the consonants are short and really are only interruptions of the steady flow of tone in order to separate the vowel sounds into words. This means that in studying tone the choir is studying vowels, and in studying purity of vowel sounds it is also studying purity of tone quality. On the other hand, it is the consonants that differentiate one word from another. They are formed by the lips, tongue, palate, teeth, and combinations of these —never the jaw. This tone interruption must be very short but must be emphasized in order cleanly to begin and terminate each syllable. The feeling of most novices will be that the consonant sound has been much exaggerated. This is because they have never made their consonants strong enough. The consonant sound should be as loud as the vowel sound itself, since it has to carry just as far in order to reach all members of the audience.

The vowels must be made pure and must be held for the full time value of the notes. The singer should feel that the breath is flowing constantly from the beginning of one breath till the next is taken, and that the tone is flowing as steadily as the breath. The consonants interrupt the flow of tone only long enough to give snap and clarity to the individual syllables. When this is done, the voices will flow smoothly, yet the enunciation will be clear and definite and every word will be understandable.

6. In congregational singing the choir should lead out confidently and joyously. The hymns are the only real opportunity the congregation has of participating actively in the service; and if the choir sings the hymns well, then the congregation will join in

freely. If necessary in order to sing them with confidence, the choir should spend time during rehearsal on the hymns to be used in the service.

Hymns should be chosen that the congregation really can sing and will enjoy singing. Then with the choir setting an inspiring tempo and instilling a spirit of enthusiasm into the music, the audience will want to join. It will be found that the singing congregation is the living congregation. When a church dies you may be sure that its music was dead first.

In the last statement we find a choir's true function. The church choir exists not for itself but for the congregation, of which it is itself a part. Only when it helps its church to have a living congregation has it achieved its destiny.

SUGGESTIONS FOR FURTHER READING

Bostrom, Otto H., Randolph, Eskil, and Johnson, Clarence A., Editors. *Anthem and Music Catalog; Arranged According to the Sundays and Special Holidays of the Church Year.* Rock Island: Augustana Book Concern, 1935. 30 pp.

An excellent catalog of choir music listed as is stated in the title. It gives the length of time needed to perform the anthem, the type of solos it contains, and the grade of its difficulty.

Cain, Noble. *Choral Music and Its Practice.* New York: M. Whitmark & Sons, 1932. 145 pp.

A book that is of most value for the director of the high school *a cappella* choir. It contains an excellent graded list of *a cappella* choir music classified according to style and period.

Coleman, Henry. *The Amateur Choir Trainer.* London: Oxford University Press, 1936. 143 pp.

An excellent book for the trainer of boys' choirs. It is, however, essentially a book dealing with voice training.

Coward, Henry. *Choral Technique and Interpretation.* London: Novello and Company, 1914. 313 pp.

An outstanding book for the conductor who must deal with advanced choral groups. The author presents the principles on which his own success has been based. In it is given a complete interpretation of *The Messiah* and the choruses of *Elijah,* as well as numerous other compositions.

Davidson, Archibald T. *Choral Conducting.* Cambridge: Harvard University Press, 1940. 73 pp.

A worth-while book dealing with problems of the amateur choir. The reader, however, needs a background of elementary conducting training before the book will benefit him greatly.

Earhart, Will. *The Eloquent Baton.* New York: M. Whitmark & Sons, 1931. 93 pp.

A book for the advanced student of conducting. The title covers the subject of the entire book—how to use the baton to the best advantage in conveying the thought of the composer to the performers following it.

Finn, William J. *The Art of the Choral Conductor.* Boston: C. C. Birchard, 1939. 292 pp.

A lengthy book based on the experiences of the author. It is excellent for the professional director, especially the trainer of boys' choirs. It is probably too long and involved and too much a book of voice training to be of great value to the amateur director of the volunteer church choir.

Gehrkins, Karl Wilson. *Essentials in Conducting.* Boston: Oliver Ditson Company, 1919. 56 pp.

An excellent book for the public school music supervisor. It deals with many types of community and school music problems and the conductor's technique in handling them.

Gehrkins, Karl Wilson. *Twenty Lessons in Conducting.* New York: Oliver Ditson Company, 1930. 63 pp.

A pocket-sized book dealing especially with baton technique. The text is well written and easily understood. Good for the beginner.

Richards, H. W. *Church Choir Training.* London: Joseph Williams, 1921. 86 pp.

A study of the volunteer boys' choir and its problems with suggestions on how to build and improve a boys' choir under adverse conditions.

Thompson, Harold W. Dickinson, Helen A., and Dickinson, Clarence. *The Choirmaster's Guide; Lists of Anthems, Solos, Services, Cantatas—Classified and Tested.* New York: H. W. Gray Company, 1924. 111 pp.

Lists of anthems, solos, and cantatas classified according to subject and seasons. The anthems listed are not analyzed or graded according to difficulty.

Wodell, F. W. *Choir and Chorus Conducting.* Philadelphia: Theodore Presser, 1902. 177 pp.

An excellent book for the conductor who wishes to broaden his knowledge of developing good choirs. The chapters are short and to the point.

INDEX

125